D0811343

Flowers

Jennifer Coldrey

Contents

Flowers everywhere

Where do flowers grow?

Plants with flowers grow nearly everywhere. People grow flowers in their gardens.

Wild flowers grow in woods, fields and hedgerows, by rivers or the sea.

Some plants, like primroses, grow best in shady places. Others, like sunflowers, prefer the sun.

Do all plants have flowers?

Most plants have flowers. Weeds and grasses have them, and so do many trees. Even vegetables like carrots and cabbages have flowers. But some plants, such as ferns, toadstools and seaweeds, have no flowers at all.

The parts of a plant

Most plants with flowers have roots, stems and leaves.

What are roots for?

Roots grow down into the soil. They hold the plant firmly in the ground. Roots also take in water from the soil. Like you, plants need water to live and grow.

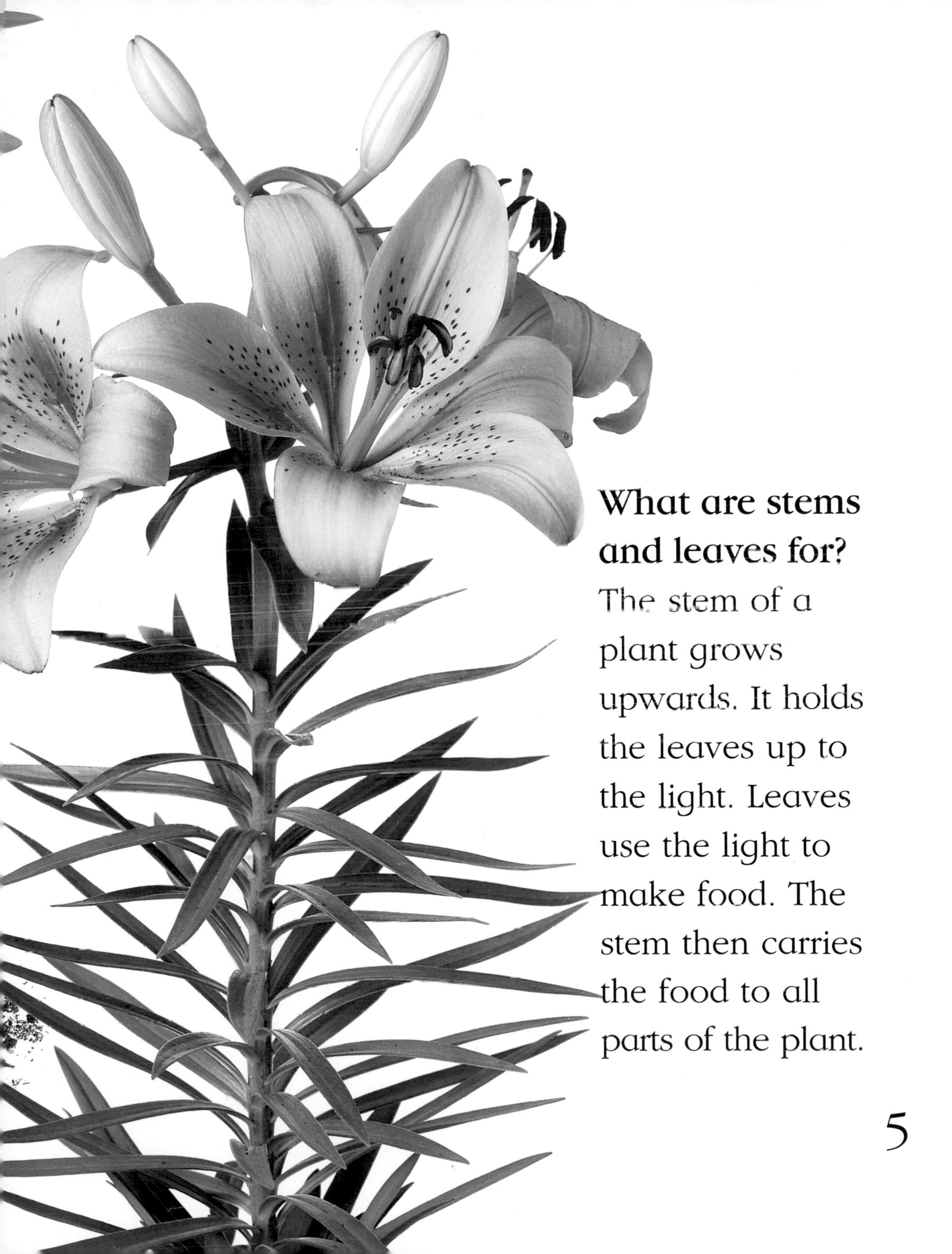

What are stems and leaves for?

The stem of a plant grows upwards. It holds the leaves up to the light. Leaves use the light to make food. The stem then carries the food to all parts of the plant.

The growing flower

Most flowers grow from buds.

What is a bud?

A bud is like a parcel. Inside, there's a young flower, folded up very, very tightly.

It's wrapped up in little green flaps called sepals, which protect it as it grows.

What happens to the bud?

Every day the bud grows a little bigger. One day, it bursts open, and the flower inside pushes out through the sepals. The petals spread out in the daylight to their full size.

The parts of a flower

A flower is made up of different parts.

A lily flower has six petals. Inside the petals is a ring of stamens. At the centre of the flower is the pistil. The pistil has a sticky top, called the stigma.

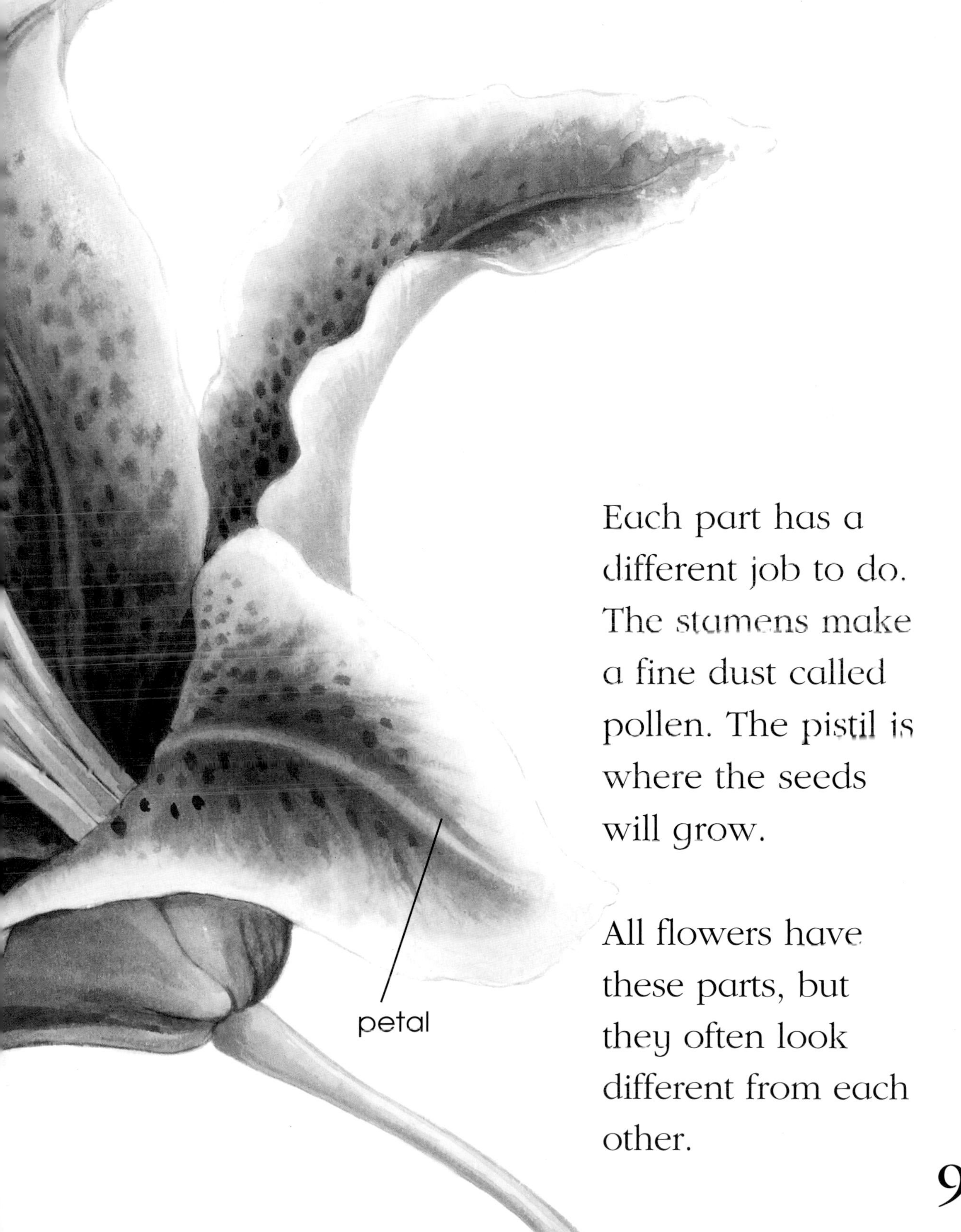

Each part has a different job to do. The stamens make a fine dust called pollen. The pistil is where the seeds will grow.

All flowers have these parts, but they often look different from each other.

Flower shapes

Flowers come in many different shapes and sizes.

Circular flowers

Flowers such as the poppy are round like a saucer. The petals are all the same size and shape. They spread out from the centre to make a circle.

Flowers like bells

Other flowers, like the bluebell, have their petals joined together to make a bell.

Different flowers

Some flowers have unusual shapes, with petals of different shapes and sizes. A sweet pea has wavy petals. Its flower looks rather like a butterfly.

Flowers on the stem

How many?

Many roses have only one flower at the top of each stem. Other plants, like hyacinths, have several flowers on a stem.

One flower or many?

The flowers on some plants grow so closely together that they look like one flower. Each tall spike of the larkspur is made up of many small flowers.

The little white flowers
of wild carrot make
big flower heads
shaped like umbrellas.

And every daisy on the
lawn is really hundreds
of tiny flowers packed
tightly together.

Flower scents

The sweet smell of a flower is called its scent. Do you like the scent of roses and hyacinths?

What makes the scent?

The scent comes from the petals or sometimes from sweet nectar hidden deep inside the flowers. On a warm day you can smell the scent of flowers on the air. Butterflies and bees smell it too.

Do all flowers smell?

Some flowers have no scent. Others smell disgusting. The giant rafflesia, the biggest flower in the world, smells like rotten meat – and flies love it!

Insect visitors

Flowers have many visitors. The visitors are usually insects, such as bees and butterflies. They spot a flower's bright colour, or they follow its sweet smell.

Why do insects visit flowers?

Flowers give food to their visitors. Bees and butterflies feed on the sweet nectar inside many flowers. They suck it up through their long, tube-like tongues.

Bees also visit flowers to collect pollen. They carry it back to their hives.

Can you see the
yellow pollen on this
honeybee's legs?

Spreading pollen

Insects help plants by spreading pollen from one flower to another. Some birds and bats do this too.

How do insects and birds spread pollen?
Look at the hummingbird feeding inside the flower. As it feeds, a few grains of pollen will rub onto its feathers. When it visits the next flower, some pollen will rub off onto the stigma.

What happens next?

When pollen grains land on the sticky stigma of a flower, the flower can begin to make seeds.

Using the wind

Not all flowers are sweet-smelling and colourful. Some plants – like grasses, nettles and many trees – have small dull flowers with no scent or nectar.

Insects don't visit these flowers. But they need to spread their pollen, too.

How do dull flowers spread their pollen?

Dull flowers use the wind to spread their pollen. Each spring the hazel tree grows long yellow catkins. The catkins are the tree's flowers. As they flutter in the breeze, their pollen is blown onto the stigmas of other hazel flowers. These flowers can then begin to make seeds.

Making seeds

How are seeds made?
When a grain of pollen lands on the stigma of a flower, it begins to grow. It grows down into the pistil, where the seeds start to develop.
The flower petals wither, but the pistil grows bigger. It slowly changes into a fruit.

All kinds of fruit

A fruit protects a plant's seeds. A fruit may be hard and dry like a nut, or soft and juicy like a tomato. Some fruits, such as the cherry, have just one seed. Others, like the poppy, have hundreds.

Spreading seeds

Plants need to spread their seeds so that new plants will grow in the future.

How do plants spread their seeds?

Plants spread their seeds in many different ways. Dandelion seeds have a fluffy parachute, and are blown far and wide on the breeze.

Poppy
seeds are
shaken
out by
the wind.

Broom seeds
are flicked
out when
their seed
pod bursts.

Animals and birds help
to spread seeds, too.
Many of them feed on
berries, and drop the
seeds that grow inside.

Desert flowers

Deserts are hot, dry places where it hardly ever rains.

How can flowers live in the desert?

All plants need water to live. Some desert plants are able to store water for a number of years. Prickly cacti store it in their plump stems. Stone plants store it in their thick leaves.

Flowers after the rain

Other desert plants have a very short life. When it rains, the waiting seeds burst open. The new plants grow, flower, make their seeds and die – all in a few short weeks.

Mountain flowers

Mountains are some of the coldest places on Earth. They have bitter winds, and snow and ice often cover the ground.

Can flowers grow here?

Many plants grow on mountains. Some grow between the rocks to shelter from the winds.

Moss campions grow in a low cushion shape, and trap warm air between their leaves.

The white edelweiss flower has woolly hairs that stop it freezing.

A short summer

Summer is short on a mountain, and flowers bloom early. They need time to make their seeds before the snow returns.

Tropical flowers

Tropical countries are hot all the year round. Rainforests grow in tropical places where there is plenty of rain.

Do flowers grow in the rainforests?

Many beautiful flowers grow in the rainforests. Some grow near the ground. Others scramble through the trees.

It is so dark here that the flowers need to be very big and very colourful. Then the birds, bats and insects can see them, and can help to spread their pollen.

Index

HarperCollins Children's Books

A Division of HarperCollins Publishers Ltd, 77–85 Fulham Palace Road, Hammersmith, London W6 8JB

First published 1994 in the United Kingdom

Copyright © HarperCollins*Publishers* 1994

All rights reserved. No part of this publication may be reproduced, stored in a retrieval system, or transmitted, in any form or by any means, electronic, mechanical, photocopying or otherwise, without the express permission of HarperCollins Publishers Ltd.

ISBN 0 00 196538 7

A CIP record is available from the British Library

Printed and bound in Hong Kong

Illustrated by Claire Jones: 19, 22; Elizabeth Rice: 16-17; Catherine Slade: 24-25, 28; Gill Tomblin: 8-9

Photographs by Brazzle Atkins: cover main image, 2-3, 10 btm; Mark Laing: 10 top, 11 btm, 21, 30, 31;

Stephen Marwood: cover top lft, btm lft, title pg, 4, 5, 6, 7, 11, 12, 13, 23; Fiona Pragoff: 14, 15 top, 24;

Bruce Coleman: 30-31 main; FLPA: 16-17; Robert Harding: 28-29; Oxford Scientific Films: 11 top lft, 13 btm rt, 15 btm, 20, 25, 26-27, 29

Series editor: Nick Hutchins; Editing: Claire Llewellyn; Design: Susi Martin;

Picture research: Liz Heasman